Copyright © 2023 Angela Marie Fertado Caragan

All rights reserved. No part of this publication may be reproduced, distributed, or transmitted in any form or by any means, including photocopying, recording, or other electronic or mechanical methods, without the prior written permission of the publisher, except in the case of brief quotations embodied in critical reviews and certain other noncommercial uses permitted by copyright law. For permission requests, contact Angela at www.angelacaragan.com.

Disclaimer: The information provided in this publication does not, and is not intended to, constitute legal, financial or tax advice; instead, all information, content, and materials are for general informational purposes only. Information may not constitute the most up-to-date legal or other information. This publication does not replace a lawyer, attorney, financial, or tax professional. The author assumes no responsibility or liability for any errors or omissions in the content. The information contained is provided on an "as is" basis with no guarantees of completeness, accuracy, usefulness, or timeliness. The reader assumes the responsibility to work with attorneys and relevant industry professionals to ensure alignment with all laws and policies related to topics contained in this publication.

ISBN: 9798530206849

THIS BOOK BELONGS TO

NAME:

PHONE:

EMAIL:

(IF IT'S LOST, YOU KNOW WHAT TO DO)

For Dad.
For Mom.
For my Mother In Love.

All who made it to the heavenly shores.

I miss you.
I love you.
Save me a seat.
I'll see you soon.

TABLE OF CONTENTS

INTRO
What am I supposed to do?   1
Getting Started   5
Self Care   11
Organization Supplies   15

TIME-BASED TASKS & CHECKLISTS
Immediately   19
Within a Few Days   23
10 Days   27
1 Month   33
3 Months   37
6 Months to 1 Year   39

FINAL THOUGHTS   45

RESOURCES
Service Outline   57
Service Considerations   59
Glossary of Terms   61

NOTEBOOK
Notes, Conversation & Task Log   69

INTRODUCTION

*Grief is like the ocean;
it comes in waves, ebbing and flowing.
Sometimes the water is calm,
and sometimes it is overwhelming.*
All we can do is learn to swim.

— *Vicki Harrison* —

WHAT AM I SUPPOSED TO DO?

What am I missing?

These were the first words that ran through my mind a few hours after my mom passed away. The cancer had finally run its course and took her life just four days before Christmas.

My father had already passed away two years prior — also from cancer. *(I hate cancer.)*

Suddenly, I realized that my sister and I were now entirely responsible for — not only the decisions about her body that we were gathered around — but also the home, property, and finances.

Talk about an overwhelming realization!
They don't teach this in college.
I genuinely didn't know where to start.

The hospital helped us with a few immediate next steps, but I still had a nagging worry *"I don't know what I don't know."* I was sure I was missing something important. The racing thoughts kept me awake for hours the following nights and weeks. The lack of sleep wasn't making handling the situation any easier.

If you ask my friends, I'm one of the most organized people they know — it's part of who I am. But then came grief, and my usually sharp mind became cloudy.

Facing the unknown while simultaneously managing a whole estate, planning a memorial, and trying to keep my life together... *It was a lot.*

WHAT AM I SUPPOSED TO DO?

In what felt like a futile attempt to wrap my head around the daunting tasks ahead, I sat down with the help of a few friends, researched, and wrote a list. It was a tally of everything that needed to get done, prioritized in order, in a rough timeline, and with loose due dates.

I've since revisited the list when others have passed away, sharing my tips with them. It's something I wish I had back in 2014 when all our minds were clouded, details were slipping through the tracks, and I was trying to survive.

I'm passing my knowledge on to you to help you in your time of loss. The sole purpose of this guideline and checklist is to help you feel a bit more organized and at peace, as you walk this journey into the unknown. It will help you keep track of crucial steps and not let tasks slip through the cracks.

The lists are **not** comprehensive as every situation and every local government varies slightly. There will be unique needs for your situation that will require you to add or eliminate from the list. If nothing else, it may guide you to find qualified professionals and ask the right questions at the meetings.

Grief is messy. While I can't organize your messy grief, I can help you manage your tasks in the middle of it. Think of this book as a gentle hand to lead you toward peace of mind and knowing you aren't missing something critically important.

So, as you walk this new journey, know that *I see you. I feel you.* This is me giving you a virtual hug and praying over you. I hope you can rest a bit easier tonight because of this guidebook.

NOTES

GETTING STARTED

If you're here, I'm going to assume you have just lost someone dear to you or are facing an imminent loss. For that, I'm so very sorry. I send you a big virtual hug and my condolences.

You are likely in a mental fog.
Things feel like a dream.

I'm afraid nothing I say right now will make it better.

So I'll tell you that...

Being in a fog is ok.
You are ok.
You will be ok.

What you are feeling is normal.

You will go through waves where sometimes you feel fine — like life is routine, and nothing has changed. Then other moments, the weight of the loss is so thick it's hard to get out of bed or shower.

That, too, is normal.

GETTING STARTED

Before we dig into the checklist, I'd like you to focus on two things throughout this process. If you don't, your journey will be that much harder.

Please start these as soon as possible:

1. TAKE CARE OF YOURSELF

What you are going through is hard, so be gentle with yourself and the loved ones around you. That's the first section of this book. But more on that in a minute.

2. WRITE EVERYTHING DOWN

Some financial and governmental processes are very complicated, so take lots and lots of notes. Over-document, so you have clear notes in a journal. Your mind is likely not as sharp, and the things you can usually easily remember will probably slip out the back.

I have provided a space throughout the book and in the back to document your notes. Use it if you'd like, or grab your favorite notebook and use my framework as a guide.

NOTES

A QUICK DISCLAIMER BEFORE YOU START

- I am not an attorney, lawyer, tax professional, or financial advisor.
- This is not meant to be legal, financial, or tax advice.
- The info is for general information purposes only.
- Things change with time, so this information may not be the most up-to-date information.
- I'm not responsible or liable for any errors or omissions in the content.
- The info is provided on an "as-is" basis.
- There is no guarantee of completeness, accuracy, usefulness, or timeliness.
- The reader assumes the responsibility to work with relevant and appropriate industry professionals to ensure alignment with all laws and policies.
- You are responsible for researching, using your professionals, and making decisions best suited for your unique situation, regardless if it aligns with the information held in this book.

SELF CARE

AS A PERSON RESPONSIBLE FOR MAKING MANY THINGS HAPPEN QUICKLY, IT'S VITAL THAT YOU CARE FOR YOUR BASIC NEEDS SO YOU CAN THINK CLEARLY AND HANDLE WHAT IS COMING YOUR WAY.

☐ Eat
Even if you don't feel like eating, have snacks throughout the day to keep your blood sugar up, so you can think clearly.
- Ask a friend to bring you some of your favorite healthy snacks to have on hand. (nuts, trail mix, fruit, string cheese, jerky, carrot sticks, granola, or protein bars)
- Bring them with you, because some appointments take longer than you expect.

☐ Drink
I don't need to tell you the importance of water.
- Grab a glass of water. *Go ahead... I'll wait.*
- Limit caffeine and energy drinks.
- Stop caffeine by mid-afternoon.
- Avoid alcoholic drinks altogether right now.

☐ Move
Getting movement will help you reset and give you a boost of the fantastic 'happy chemicals' (*hello, dopamine and endorphins*). Try taking a few breaks throughout the day, moving in a way that feels best to you and is something you enjoy.
- Take a short walk or go for a bike ride.
- Grab a workout or yoga class online or in person.
- Hit the gym.
- Play outside with the kids.
- Have a dance party.

SELF CARE

☐ # Sleep

Prioritize your sleep and try to calm your mind. Rest is essential for decision-making. Your mind may race at night with everything you have to do, all the emotions, memories, and even regrets.

- Use a sound machine or white noise.
- Listen to a sleep story or meditation. There are many apps, such as Calm or Abide.
- Listen to soothing instrumental music.
- If needed, take an over-the-counter sleep aid or ask your doctor for a prescription if natural or other remedies aren't helping. While you may not want to take it long-term, it might be beneficial for a short-term solution.

☐ # Get Help

You will need to manage your household, family, and job while taking on this new responsibility. You cannot do this alone. People will offer to help, so accept it and return the favor in their time of need. If they offer a vague "let me know if you need help," thank them and be specific with what they can do for you — even if it's small. Sit down and write a list of things that you could use help with so that when someone asks, you can grab your list and ask for something specific.

- Let your friends or church family set up meal delivery.
- Ask someone to watch your kids.
- Get someone to go grocery shopping.
- Have someone mow your lawn or fold your laundry.
- Ask someone to just sit with you while you do other tasks.
- Hire a therapist.
- Talk to a pastor or a mentor.

NOTES

ORGANIZATION SUPPLIES

HERE ARE A FEW RECOMMENDATIONS TO HELP YOU STAY ORGANIZED

☐ **Notepad and Pen**
Keep it nearby and bring it with you to all appointments. Your mind will be a bit what I call "mushy" right now. Details may get lost or forgotten if you don't write everything down.

☐ **Folders or Manila Envelopes**
Even in the digital age, you will have a lot of paper. Keep everything together by categorizing by type of correspondence (bank, investments, death certificates, home insurance, car insurance, house deed, etc.).

☐ **Portable File Box or Accordion File Organizer**
You can keep your folders organized by having them in a single location — a go-to box — so you don't have to look for things.

☐ **Download Printable Checklists & Forms**
Get downloadable to-do lists, notes, and call log templates:
ANGELACARAGAN.COM/WHATTODO

TIME-BASED TASKS

IMMEDIATELY

☐ Get an Official Declaration of Death

- Notify the person's doctor and/or local coroner.
- If the person passes away in the hospital, hospital staff will usually contact the right people. However, you may want to ask.
- The local law enforcement agency must be notified if the person passes away elsewhere (such as at home). They likely will come to the house or location where the person died to validate that there was no criminal activity. They may ask you to leave the area so they can do their investigation. This may feel awkward and business-like. They are doing it to ensure no foul play and to clear the family of any possible accusations.

☐ Notify Close Family and Friends

- Call the people who need to hear it directly from you.
- Ask or delegate someone else to contact others and have them field the onslaught of questions and phone calls that will come.
- Only share what you're comfortable sharing. Likely everyone will want to hear all the details. You are not obligated to answer all their questions and tell the story repeatedly. You are empowered to hold boundaries to guard your mental health. Have a few phrases at the ready such as "I don't have the energy to tell the story right now." Send them to your delegate if that feels like a better solution.

IMMEDIATELY

☐ Arrange for Organ Donation
- If the deceased or family wished to donate their organs, work with the medical professionals on the appropriate next steps.

☐ Handle Care of Dependants and Pets
- Find a reliable friend or professional to take on any dependents or pets.

☐ Call the Person's Employer, if They Were Working
- Request info about benefits and any pay due.
- Ask whether there was a life insurance policy through the company.
- Ask if anything is needed to close their employment (such as returning equipment, etc.)

ADD YOUR OWN:

☐

☐

☐

☐

NOTES

WITHIN A FEW DAYS

☐ **Make Arrangements for Funeral, Burial or Cremation**
- Look through the person's documents to find out whether there was a prepaid burial plan.
- If there are no prepaid plans, select a funeral home and mortuary. When choosing, ask detailed questions about costs to help with your budget.
- Make arrangements for the mortuary to collect the body. The hospital may need a signature or verbal permission to release the body into the care of the mortuary. If at home, the mortuary/funeral home/morgue will arrange to pick up the body.
- Set an appointment time with the mortuary to meet with the director to fill out documentation, make decisions, sign, and pay. Ask a friend or family member to go with you. Payment or partial payment is usually expected at the time of the meeting.

☐ **Gather the Deceased's Information**

This will be needed for the funeral home and death certificate. Gather this before your meeting at the funeral home. If you need clarification, call the closest relatives who can help answer the questions. Brothers and sisters, birth and marriage certificates can answer most.

- Full Name
- Date of Birth
- Date of Death
- Social Security Number
- Location of Birth
- Spouse's Name
- Parent's Full Names
- Nationality
- Address
- Occupation
- Military Status

WITHIN A FEW DAYS

☐ Find the Person's Estate Plan, Will, Trust, and Executor

- Read through it to find any specific requests about funeral arrangements, individuals, and responsibilities.
- Keep this with your file organizer and bring it to your appointments.

☐ Prepare an Obituary

In the digital era, an obituary is not as often published in newspapers, but funeral homes or local newspapers sometimes post a digital copy for a fee. Even if you don't intend to print the obituary, many people still use the written words to share via social media, post on a website, or read at the funeral or memorial service. Articles on how to write an obituary can be easily found online if you need ideas.

☐ Contact the Person's Organizations

Contact that organization if they were in the military or belonged to a fraternal or religious group. The group may have benefits or will assist with conducting services.

☐ Create a Rough Budget

- Arrangements can be expensive when someone passes, depending on how fancy the plans are.
- Funeral homes will sometimes play on emotions and encourage the "best" for the passed loved one, which is code for paid add-ons. You'll need to decide what is practical for your situation and finances. There is a list of typical expense elements in the service elements section at the back of this guidebook to help you start drafting your budget items.

☐ Ask Someone to Keep an Eye on the Person's Home

- Visit the home occasionally to collect mail and newspapers and make the house look lived-in.
- Clean out any perishables from the refrigerator.
- Put out the garbage on weekly collection days.
- Call the non-emergency line for the local Police department and ask them to periodically check on the house (please do not call 911 for this).

☐ Start a Thank You List

- Keep track of all donations, flowers, helping hands, cards and meals received.
- Don't forget to include any hospital, hospice, or nursing care staff who may have helped ease the pain of loss.

ADD YOUR OWN:

☐

☐

☐

☐

UP TO 10 DAYS

☐ Obtain Death Certificates
- The funeral home usually supplies certificates for a fee.
- Get 6-8 certified copies. Most financial institutions, government agencies, and insurers will need an original certified document.
- Additional certified copies can be ordered later from the funeral home or your local government and county.

☐ Notify, Cancel, Stop, or Pause Services
- Utility companies if the home will not be in use (Gas, Electric, Water, Sewer, etc.)
- Internet or Cable Companies
- Newspapers and Magazines
- Online or Streaming Subscription Services (such as Hulu, Amazon, Netflix, Audible, etc.)
- Cell Phone — Consider forwarding the number to a relative.
- Car Insurance
- Health Insurance
- Home or Renters Insurance — Change the name on the policy or cancel once no longer in possession.

☐ Document All Financial Transactions and Receipts
- Start a spreadsheet of all financial transactions you may do on the Estate's behalf, especially if someone paid personally and needs a reimbursement. Notes who, what, when, and status of the transaction (for example, if a refund is outstanding vs. paid).
- Organize, file, and keep all receipts.

UP TO 10 DAYS

☐ **Find and Book an Appointment with a Reputable Trust and Estate Attorney**
- Ask friends and family if the deceased had someone they preferred, or ask for personal recommendations.
- This professional will help you with the appropriate steps, paperwork, and all laws. They will assist you with transferring assets and actions concerning the Trust or Probate.
- This is especially important if there is no Trust and the Estate has to go to Probate. You will want a professional to guide you through the legalities.
- Bring a trusted friend or relative to the appointment for a second pair of ears and support you.

☐ **Take the Will to Probate, if there is no Trust**

Work with your estate attorney on the specifics of probate procedures.
- Obtain Letters of Testamentary or Letters of Administration. Obtain these from the local courthouse or city hall in the county where the deceased lived when they died.
- You may need to take the official will to the courthouse, along with a certified death certificate, and file a probate petition.
- Once the court opens a probate file and validates the will, it gives you the authority (via the letters testamentary) to carry out the duties required to settle the estate and act on behalf of the deceased in accordance with the person's will.

UP TO 10 DAYS

☐ Get an EIN Number for the Estate

The EIN Number is the identifying number for all financial transactions. It's like a Social Security Number or a Business License Number that allows the Trust to operate as its own entity. Getting one is a straightforward process online.
- Document the EIN Number with the Estate notes and documents for all future use.
- If only one spouse has died, the EIN may not be needed until both have passed away.
- This number will be needed for tax returns.

☐ Open a Bank Account for the Estate

- The EIN, Death Certificate, and Estate Documentation (will, trust, power of attorney, etc.) will be needed to open this account.
- All financial transactions should be done in the new account, such as house payments, funeral home payments, etc.

☐ Contact Financial & Insurance Institutions

Many of these will require the death certificate, notarized power of attorney paperwork, or estate executor or beneficiary documentation to gain access.
- The person's investment advisor for information on holdings. *Do not make decisions immediately until you thoroughly understand your options and the implications.*
- The bank to find accounts and a safe deposit box.
- Credit cards to cancel and pay off debt. Note: Most large credit card companies will forgive the outstanding debt.
- Life insurance agent to get claim forms.
- Insurance companies such as for their home, car, etc.
- A tax advisor or CPA to get the necessary next steps.

29

UP TO 10 DAYS

☐ Contact Financial Institutions and Individuals (cont.)

- Social Security (socialsecurity.gov) to stop payment and ask about survivor benefits. Some funeral homes will notify Social Security directly. Make sure Social Security has informed the credit reporting companies.
- Other agencies from which the deceased received benefits, such as Veterans Affairs (va.gov), stop payment and ask about survivor benefits.
- Notify DMV and cancel the driver's license.
- Agency providing pension services to stop monthly checks and get claim forms.
- Contact all creditors with whom the deceased person did business and request that they mark their files accordingly. They may need the death certificate once you receive it.
- Credit companies (Experian, Equifax, TransUnion) to notify of the death and instruct them to list all accounts as: "Closed. Account Holder is Deceased.". Check to see if they need the death certificate.
- Update voter registration

ADD YOUR OWN:

☐

☐

☐

NOTES

UP TO 1 MONTH

☐ **Make a List of Bills and Continue to Pay All Bills and Services**

Pay bills, as needed, through the estate account until services have been canceled and the estate has been distributed to the beneficiaries and closed.

☐ **Collect the Following Documents**

Keep these for your records and to use as needed to manage the estate while things are in progress.
- The death certificate(s).
- If both spouses have passed, you will need both individuals' death certificates.
- The will or trust
- Insurance policies (life, homeowners, health, disability, auto, etc.)
- Last credit card statements
- Investment accounts (IRAs, 401k plans, mutual funds, pensions, stock certificates, etc.)
- Last checking and savings account statements (including CDs and money-market accounts)
- Last mortgage statement
- Last two years' tax returns
- Marriage and birth certificates
- An up-to-date credit report of the deceased
- Social security card(s)

UP TO 1 MONTH

☐ **List Deceased Name on the Deceased Do Not Contact List**
For a small fee, you can list the decedent's name on the "Deceased Do Not Contact List," which is maintained by the Direct Marketing Association (www.ims-dm.com/cgi/ddnc).

☐ **Request Mail Forwarding by USPS**
Forward to the Estate Executor or a Beneficiary.

☐ **Send Thank You Notes**
- Purchase Thank You cards or Sympathy Acknowledgement cards and send them to your list.
- Consider sending a small gift, such as a gift card, for anyone that went above and beyond during this time.

ADD YOUR OWN:

☐

☐

☐

☐

☐

NOTES

UP TO 3 MONTHS

☐ Find and List all Assets

Start documenting all the items of value, both physical and liquid assets. You will likely need this when you distribute assets.

☐ Clean Out Belongings or Pack / Store

When cleaning belongings out, organize items into four categories:
- **Friends & Family wish to keep** — Treat this with emotional care, as multiple people may want the same things. Develop a negotiation strategy or bring in a neutral third party to help mediate and negotiate.
- **Donate** — Many places, like the Vietnam Veterans of America, will do scheduled pickups, so you don't have to haul it yourself.
- **Sell** — There are many online ways to sell. You could even ask a friend to sell it on your behalf and give them a small thank-you gift or a commission.
- **Garbage** — Most garbage services offer a few large items or extra pickups throughout the year at no additional costs. The rest can be taken to a dump or pay a junk pickup service. Shred all financial and confidential documents.

ADD YOUR OWN:

☐

☐

UP TO 6 MONTHS TO 1 YEAR

☐ **Sell the House or Transfer the Deed to a Family Member**
- Get the house professionally appraised to understand the value of the home.
- Work with a realtor, local attorney, and tax professional to understand the best process before starting any paperwork. *(See the note on transferring assets below)*

☐ **Transfer and Distribute Assets**
- Distribute liquid assets by dividing bank accounts.
- IRAs or retirement accounts - Make sure you understand the Required Minimum Distributions (RMDs) and tax implications when making decisions about investments.
- Divide up any remaining personal belongings and sell or donate the rest.

NOTE ON TRANSFERRING ASSETS

*Find a great estate attorney **and** tax professional who understands local law.*

How you do this can be very important and have a financial impact.

For example, in some states, property taxes are not reassessed and are increased if the property goes straight from a parent to the child. If one of the children wants to keep the home, it might be better to transfer the house directly to one child and give the other child equivalent valued liquid assets such as Retirement Accounts, Savings, or Checking funds.

See an example of why this matters on the next page...

UP TO 6 MONTHS TO 1 YEAR

TRANSFERRING ASSETS EXAMPLE:

Mom just passed away and is the last remaining parent.

Mom and Dad had two adult children, Susan and Bob, who inherited everything 50%/50% through a trust. Susan wants the family home, and Bob is okay with her having it as long as assets and the home value is distributed evenly.

House value = $500,000
Cash in Bank = $200,000
Retirement Account = $300,000

The total valuation is $1 million, giving $500k to each child.

OPTION 1: Split everything equally
(which at face value sounds easiest and best)

- Transfer the house deed from Mom and Dad or Trust to Susan and Bob's name. There is no tax reassessment through the trust and inheritance, so taxes will be paid on the $60k amount Mom and Dad bought it for 40 years ago.
- Susan gives Bob $250k to buy him out of his half of the house.
- The House deed moves from Susan & Bob's names to only Susan's name. This triggers a property tax assessment at a current value of $500k because now it's going from child to child.
- Split the cash and retirement and give them $100k and $150k each.

RESULT: They still both get their $500k value. But now, Susan has higher property taxes to pay each year.

TRANSFERRING ASSETS EXAMPLE (CONT):

OPTION 2: Give Susan the house and give Bob the cash & retirement accounts

- Transfer the house deed from Mom and Dad or Trust to directly to Susan's name alone. There is no tax reassessment through the trust and inheritance, so taxes will be paid on the $60k amount Mom and Dad bought it for 40 years ago.
- Bob takes all the cash and retirement accounts.

RESULT: They still both get their $500k value, but now Susan will pay the property taxes on the house value from when Mom and Dad bought it at $60k 40 years ago.

NOTE ON TRANSFERRING INVESTMENT / RETIREMENT ACCOUNTS

*The rules about what you must pull out and when or how it's distributed can be complicated and have tax implications. I've found that most financial institutions will show you the options but won't advise you to make the best decision because that is out of their scope. Use your tax professional, a financial advisor, **and** the financial investment institution to determine what is best for you so you don't get any penalties or significantly pay higher taxes.*

CONCLUSION:

You must do detailed math to determine exact values and what is fair and makes the most sense. Do not make moves or decisions without fully exploring all the options with attorneys and tax professionals!

Please don't do it alone! Use your professionals!

UP TO 6 MONTHS TO 1 YEAR

☐ **Close and Cancel Any Outstanding Recurring Bills or Accounts**
- Cancel home or renters insurance (once the home is no longer in the posession of the trust or beneficiaries)
- Utility companies (Gas, Electric, Water, Sewer, etc.)
- Insurance policies remaining
- Financial accounts

☐ **Close Email and Online Accounts**

Close and cancel all known email and online accounts to prevent fraud.

☐ **Delete or Memorialize Social Media Accounts**

It's a good idea to either memorialize or deactivate the accounts. Each social media entity has its own process and required documentation. Write a list of all the known social media accounts and work through the process for each.

☐ **File the Will at the Courthouse, if not in probate**

Many counties and states require this step to be done. This is even if you have a trust, and the will doesn't say anything besides 'refer back to the trust.'

☐ **File a Final Tax Return**

This will need to be filed on behalf of the deceased. Your CPA or tax preparer can advise if you need to do this and can help you make the appropriate filing type.

☐ Close the Estate Bank Account
All financial books should reflect zero balance.

☐ Close the Estate
Usually, your CPA will file the appropriate files with the last tax return to consider the estate closed. Work with your CPA and attorney to ensure the estate is considered "closed."

NOTE ABOUT CLOSING THE ESTATE

Depending on the complexity of the estate and the local state laws, how long it takes to settle and close the estate could take anywhere from 6 months to 3 years. Some states require you to close the Trust and settle an estate by a specific time. When I went through it, it was 3 years from the date of death. Check current rules and plan accordingly.

☐

☐

☐

☐

☐

FINAL THOUGHTS

*Grief is the last act of love
we have to give to those we loved.
**Where there is deep grief,
there was great love.***

— *Anonymous* —

GET YOUR AFFAIRS IN ORDER

One of the final gifts my parents gave me beyond the grave was an estate and finances that were in order.

Please don't delay if you haven't completed your estate plan and got your affairs in order.

I know it's not something any of us want to think about. However, ignoring it doesn't change the fact that someday, death will come for all of us.

Get the following set up as soon as you can:

- **Estate Plan.**
    - Last Will & Testament
    - Durable Power of Attorney
    - Financial Power of Attorney
    - Medical Power of Attorney
    - Revocable Living Trust
    - Advance Healthcare Directive
- **Life Insurance**
- **Written Plan of your Wishes**

Do it for the sake of the loved ones that someday will need to do all these tasks for you.

YOU WILL GET THROUGH THIS

You are going to be okay.
You are going to get through this.
It may not feel like it right now, but you will.

You are good enough to do this work.
You are worthy.
You are valued.
You are important
You are loved.

Breathe.
Pray.
Hug someone.
Repeat.

I believe in you.
You got this.

Much love to you,
Angela

THANK YOU TO

God for everything.

*My husband, Eddie,
for loving me deeply, supporting me,
and walking this path with me.*

*My sister, Robin,
for being the best co-trustee and
friend in our monumental loss.*

*My dog, Laila,
for becoming a 'mental health dog'
and excelling in the role.*

*My friends & family
for being kind, prayerful,
understanding, and cheering me on.*

RESOURCES

RESOURCES

SAMPLE SERVICE OUTLINE

1. Prelude Music
2. Opening Prayer
3. Scripture Reading
4. Obituary
5. Song
6. Testimonials
7. Photo Slideshow Video
8. Minister's Message
9. Closing Prayer
10. Postlude Music

SERVICE CONSIDERATIONS

- Choice of Funeral Home – $
- Service Location
- Service Date & Time
- Special View Date & Time
- Interment Following? If so, what location?
- Ministers involved – $ *donation*
- Speakers
- Obituary – $
- Music & Special Songs – $ *donation*
- Slideshow Video
- Picture & Memorial Display – $
- Military Honors Service
- Order of Service
- Pallbearers
- Ushers
- Printed Programs/Bulletins – $
- Flowers - Consider delegating someone to move them between viewing, funeral, burial, and reception – $
- Printed directions to the burial and/or reception – $
- Reception Plans
    - Location – $
    - Food – $
    - Decor – $
    - Clean Up

$ - Typically incurs costs

GLOSSARY OF TERMS

BURIAL & SERVICES

Burial - also known as interment or inhumation, is a method of final disposition by placing a dead body or ashes into the ground.

Casket - a burial container used to hold the remains of the deceased for burial or interment. Most caskets are made of wood — some plain and others more ornamental. They have a hinged lid and rails to make transportation and carrying easier.

Coffin - a burial container used to hold the deceased's remains for burial with a removable lid. Coffins are usually made out of wood and lined with cloth interiors. Unlike caskets, they do not have rails for transportation. Coffins get tapered to conform to the shape of a human form and are less preferred to caskets.

Columbarium - a room or building with niches for storing funeral urns.

Cremation - the disposal of a dead person's body by burning it to ashes. Family can take the ashes to scatter, place them in an urn and display them at home, or do an interment in the ground or a columbarium.

Eulogy - a speech or writing that talks about a person who has just died and generally praises them. Sometimes, a eulogy includes telling their basic story - origins, family, marriage, main accomplishments, etc.

Funeral Service - a service where the body is present, often in a casket in a place of honor. The service usually includes things such as the presence of a casket, religious rituals (if applicable), and post-funeral burial.

GLOSSARY | BURIIAL & SERVICES

Graveside Service - a service of remembrance and celebration for the deceased's life at the site of the burial niche or plot, usually led by a pastor. It is often held immediately following the funeral, or if the memorial service is held later, the graveside service may be conducted shortly after the death as an independent event.

Interment of Ashes - when cremated remains are buried in the ground or placed in a building designed to hold ashes, known as a columbarium. This is an option if you prefer to avoid scattering them or display them in an urn in your home.

Interment of a Casket - the ceremonial placing of a deceased person in a grave. A body in a casket or coffin can be interred.

Mausoleum - a building, usually large and somewhat stately, that houses the deceased in a casket or coffin. It can hold a single casket or multiple.

Memorial Service - a service where the body is not present, though there may be an urn or a photograph of the deceased as a central focus.

Mortuary - a service provider offering management of the body of the recently deceased person, including embalming and on-site cremation. Sometimes referred to as a funeral home.

Morgue - storage spaces for bodies until they are claimed or redirected. Often found in hospitals or at mortuaries/funeral homes.

GLOSSARY | BURIIAL & SERVICES

Niche - a space in a mausoleum or columbarium where an urn or container holding cremated remains are placed.

Obituary - a formal announcement of a death often printed in a newspaper. It typically includes a brief biography of the deceased. Some obituaries are published online or are read at a funeral.

Pallbearer - a person who helps carry the casket or coffin at a funeral. It is common for six strong family members or friends to be selected for pallbearing duties.

GLOSSARY OF TERMS

ESTATE & LEGAL

Advance Healthcare Directive - a legal document that explains how you want medical decisions about you to be made if you cannot make the decisions yourself. An advance directive lets your healthcare team and loved ones know what kind of healthcare you want or whom you want to decide when you can't.

Beneficiary - anyone you name in your Estate Plan who will ultimately benefit from your estate in the form of money or assets.

Estate - all the money and property owned by a particular person, typically referred to as an Estate at death.

Estate Plan - a set of legal documents that present your wishes for the distribution of property, guardianship of minor children, and even healthcare decisions. An Estate Planning attorney can help draw up these plans and ensure the appropriate documents are included.

Executor - the person who administers a person's estate upon their death. The primary duty is to carry out the wishes of the deceased person based on instructions spelled out in their will or trust documents, ensuring that assets are distributed to the intended beneficiaries.

Fiduciary - a person or organization that acts on behalf of another person or persons, putting their client's interests ahead of their own, with a duty to preserve good faith and trust. Being a fiduciary thus requires being legally and ethically bound to act in the other's best interests. An executor of a will or estate is considered a Fiduciary. An attorney is also a fiduciary.

GLOSSARY | ESTATE & LEGAL

Power of Attorney / Durable Power of Attorney - a way to allow someone else to manage someone's finances in the event they become incapacitated and unable to make those decisions themselves.

Power of Attorney / Financial Power of Attorney - allows someone to manage their financial matters, keeping track of everything and managing affairs in the event the person becomes incapacitated and cannot do it themselves.

Power of Attorney / Medical Power of Attorney - allows someone to grant a trusted person, known as an agent, the authority to make medical and end-of-life care decisions on their behalf.

Trust / Revocable Living Trust *(more common and recommended)* - a popular estate planning tool that lets a person control how their property is handled during their life and after death. It also helps avoid probate and transfers their property quickly and privately.

Trust / Irrevocable Living Trust *(rare)* - a type of trust where its terms cannot be modified, amended or terminated without the grantor's beneficiary's or beneficiaries' permission. Having effectively transferred all ownership of assets into the trust, the grantor legally removes all of their rights of ownership to the assets and the trust. Irrevocable trusts are generally set up to minimize estate taxes, access government benefits, and protect assets. This is in contrast to a revocable trust, which allows the grantor to modify the trust, but loses certain benefits such as creditor protection.

GLOSSARY | ESTATE & LEGAL

Trustee - A trustee takes legal ownership of the assets held by a trust and assumes fiduciary responsibility for managing those assets and carrying out the purposes of the trust.

Will / Last Will and Testament - a legal document stating their preferences about how their estates should be handled after their death.

NOTEBOOK

NOTES

NOTES

NOTES

NOTES

NOTES

NOTES

NOTES

NOTES

NOTES

NOTES

NOTES

CONVERSATION & TASK LOG

COMPANY:

DATE:

NAME:

PHONE/EMAIL:

NOTES:

NEXT STEPS & TO-DO'S:

DATE:

NAME:

PHONE/EMAIL:

NOTES:

NEXT STEPS & TO-DO'S:

CONVERSATION & TASK LOG

COMPANY:

DATE: NAME: PHONE/EMAIL:

NOTES: NEXT STEPS & TO-DO'S:

DATE: NAME: PHONE/EMAIL:

NOTES: NEXT STEPS & TO-DO'S:

CONVERSATION & TASK LOG

COMPANY:

DATE: NAME: PHONE/EMAIL:

NOTES: NEXT STEPS & TO-DO'S:

DATE: NAME: PHONE/EMAIL:

NOTES: NEXT STEPS & TO-DO'S:

CONVERSATION & TASK LOG

COMPANY:

DATE: NAME: PHONE/EMAIL:

NOTES: NEXT STEPS & TO-DO'S:

DATE: NAME: PHONE/EMAIL:

NOTES: NEXT STEPS & TO-DO'S:

CONVERSATION & TASK LOG

COMPANY:

DATE: NAME: PHONE/EMAIL:

NOTES: NEXT STEPS & TO-DO'S:

DATE: NAME: PHONE/EMAIL:

NOTES: NEXT STEPS & TO-DO'S:

CONVERSATION & TASK LOG

COMPANY:

DATE: NAME: PHONE/EMAIL:

NOTES: NEXT STEPS & TO-DO'S:

DATE: NAME: PHONE/EMAIL:

NOTES: NEXT STEPS & TO-DO'S:

CONVERSATION & TASK LOG

COMPANY:

DATE:

NAME:

PHONE/EMAIL:

NOTES:

NEXT STEPS & TO-DO'S:

DATE:

NAME:

PHONE/EMAIL:

NOTES:

NEXT STEPS & TO-DO'S:

CONVERSATION & TASK LOG

COMPANY:

DATE:

NAME:

PHONE/EMAIL:

NOTES:

NEXT STEPS & TO-DO'S:

DATE:

NAME:

PHONE/EMAIL:

NOTES:

NEXT STEPS & TO-DO'S:

CONVERSATION & TASK LOG

COMPANY:

DATE: NAME: PHONE/EMAIL:

NOTES: NEXT STEPS & TO-DO'S:

DATE: NAME: PHONE/EMAIL:

NOTES: NEXT STEPS & TO-DO'S:

CONVERSATION & TASK LOG

COMPANY:

DATE:

NAME:

PHONE/EMAIL:

NOTES:

NEXT STEPS & TO-DO'S:

DATE:

NAME:

PHONE/EMAIL:

NOTES:

NEXT STEPS & TO-DO'S:

ABOUT THE AUTHOR

Angela lives with her husband Eddie and dog Laila in Northern California.

She works as a Digital Experience Strategist and volunteers her time with a local church facilitating administrative operations and church experiences.

Raised in an entrepreneur and pastor's home, Angela learned early on the importance of hard work and helping others.

That is why she is passionate about helping people - spiritually, mentally, and physically.

www.angelacaragan.com

Photo by GemaLuna Photography

Made in the USA
Coppell, TX
14 April 2024